Listening to Nature's Voice

reflections on the world around us

Pamela Baxter

Hidden Oasis Publishing • Kimberton, PA

Also by Pamela Baxter

HIDDEN OASIS PUBLISHING

On Grandpa's Beach in Maine

Big Life Lessons from Nature's Little Secrets

Explore Outdoors, a Nature Journal for Kids

SKINNER HOUSE BOOKS

A Cup of Light

FRONT COVER PHOTO BY Elaine Lang Cornett

PUBLISHED BY

Hidden Oasis Publishing

P.O. Box 80

Kimberton, PA 19442

www.PamelaBaxterBooks.com

Paperback ISBN 978-0-9884636-4-6
Library of Congress Control Number: 2024924597

instructions for living a life

pay attention

be astonished

tell about it

—mary oliver

preface

"I saw this today and thought you might enjoy seeing it too."

During an especially spectacular fall season in New England, a friend who lives in Maine posted a photo update on her social media. The image showed a crimson-leaved Virginia creeper vine ranging over a jumble of lichen-covered stones. In the comments below the post another friend had written, *"Thank you for taking the time to notice the small things, so that we can enjoy them as well!"*

Those words spoke to me because I have spent a lifetime noticing little things in nature and trying to find ways to share them with others. While the world is filled with amazing things, not everyone has the time or inclination to stop and look at elements that are less obvious but no less remarkable. The little things I notice often find their way onto my own social media and into my garden column. It's my way of saying, "I saw this today and thought you might enjoy seeing it too."

Some years ago, however, I noticed something beyond visual beauty and general interest. I found that many of the things that I observed in nature contained messages that gave me guidance, strength, and even inspiration. My book for children, *"Big Life Lessons from Nature's Little Secrets"* explores thirty-one such "messages." Following each entry, I included a series of targeted questions designed to get kids to think about their own life experiences and to see how the way things work in nature could help give them direction.

The reviews I received were gratifying, including queries from parents asking if I would consider writing a similar book for adults. This book is the result. I hope that you will find the essays engaging and that in reflecting on the questions I've posed you'll discover wisdom you can apply to your own life. I also hope that the essays will inspire you to experience and think about our natural environment in a different way, and to see it through a new, more deeply personal lens.

Pamela Baxter
November 2024

table of contents

1 **a scene from the lorax**
   finding inspiration 1

2 **crouching gardener, hidden spider**
   seeing our own beauty 5

3 **a patch of moss**
   noticing small things 9

4 **tomato plants**
   reaching for your goals 13

5 **the fox i didn't see**
   keeping our eyes open 17

6 **hickory nuts**
   letting things go 21

7 **are we there yet?**
   approaching the summit 25

8 **barefoot in the garden**
   staying grounded 29

9 **the sentience of trees**
   being connected 33

10 **the star in an apple**
   changing perspective 37

11 **empty spaces**
making room.. 41

12 **redbud trees**
seeding dreams..45

13 **a lesson from a caterpillar**
creating a support system.....................................49

14 **the old oak tree**
aging with grace...53

15 **the mud dauber wasp**
being persistent.. 57

16 **the walnut shell**
doing what we can... 61

17 **stuck on a mountainside**
creating a buffer..65

18 **spiders in the window**
finding a niche..69

19 **the story of a seed**
setting intentions 73

20 **the gift of rain**
making the most of the day...................................77

21 the promise of seeds
growing where you're planted 81

22 the ruby-throated hummingbird
being in the right place 85

23 a colony of ants
the art of communicating 89

24 the view from the hilltop
getting perspective 93

25 sending probes into space
starting a project 97

26 flowers along the creek
choosing our words 101

27 "esther williams" goes for a swim
making assumptions 105

28 sunrise on vero beach
greeting the day 109

29 botanical rivals
moving up in the world 113

30 what's the end?
flowering like a tree 117

1

a scene from *the lorax*
finding inspiration

I hadn't seen my friend Mary Ann in a while. As I approached her house, I found her street-side garden abundant with spider plants (*Cleome hassleriana*) and clematis. It was the end of summer, and the clematis vines were laden with tousled-looking seed whorls, their champagne-colored tufts spiraled like little mop-heads.

The cleome was tall enough to be nearly at my eye level. Swaying a bit at the tips of their stalks, the flowers seemed to lean their heads toward me, like near-sighted people straining to see better. Below the flowers were tiers of the signature, branching seed pods that inspire some people to call this plant "Grandfather's Whiskers."

Looking at the clematis and the cleome I wondered if children's author Dr. Seuss had ever seen these species. (Compare a photo of clematis seed heads and an illustration from *The Lorax*, and you'll see what I mean.) I had always thought that Seuss just had a wild imagination; was it possible that the inspiration for his zany-looking creatures came from the natural world around him?

Other examples of possible art-from-nature come to mind. For instance, the writing spider (*Argiope aurantia*) I discovered at the back of the house one day. I was fascinated by the bold, zig-zag pattern that decorated its web and I wondered if author E.B. White had ever seen such a thing. Could a writing spider have been the inspiration for White's classic children's book, *Charlotte's Web*?

Years ago, when I was learning how to play the bagpipes, I was intrigued to find ornaments* that sounded like birdsong; in particular, the sweet cadence of the wood thrush. Had birds inspired pipers of old to try and mimic these sounds? Why not? Composer Ludwig van Beethoven was known to take frequent walks in the countryside surrounding the city of Vienna. Many of the sounds of nature—e.g., birdsong and thunderstorms—emerge in his sixth symphony, dubbed the *Pastoral*, just as they do in Vivaldi's famous orchestral work, *The Four Seasons*.

*In bagpipe music, ornaments are the combination of embellishments that give pipe music its distinctive "burbly" sound.

You don't need to be an artist or musician to be influenced by the natural world. Nature can inspire or inhabit what we do without us being actively aware of it. It has obviously inspired this book of reflections and questions. Pretty much everything that I see, hear, taste, and touch influences how I experience the world and how I act in it.

i find myself wondering . . .

Since environment tends to shape our thoughts, behaviors, and creativity, doesn't it make sense to provide ourselves with the best environment we can either find or make for ourselves?

take a few moments to reflect . . .

Where, physically, do you find inspiration? Can you spend more time there?

Is your immediate environment inspiring or deadening?

What might make it more enlivening— a fresh coat of paint? Getting rid of clutter?

crouching gardener, hidden spider

seeing our own beauty

A flicker of gold caught my eye as I picked wilted daylily blossoms off their stems. I looked closer and saw a spider, barely half an inch long, crouched in the cup of one of the bright orange flowers still fully open. The spider's tiny body was iridescent gold, like one of the priceless artifacts sealed up in King Tut's tomb. An unmistakable defensive posture that kept the spider facing me as I moved told me that the spider knew I was there, observing it from all angles.

The spider's beauty captivated me, and I wondered what kind it was. What was its scientific name? There are so many spiders in the world; had anyone ever seen this one before? Probably. But my mind was mostly occupied with wondering why the spider was so lavishly adorned. What purpose did the brilliant, glinting, gold color serve?

Here was this small member of the Arachnid family, out trapping food and doing whatever else spiders do during the day. Regardless of what it was up to, I'm certain that the spider had no idea of its beauty and could not comprehend that someone would stop to notice it as being worth more than a quick snack.

Who knows? Perhaps the moment with the spider was just to catch my attention, for me to be more fully present. Maybe the moment was to let me see a spider as something other than scary.

Only a few of us live highly-noticeable lives— winning a gold medal, writing a best seller, finding a cure, brokering peace, having thousands of followers on social media, or captivating audiences from the silver screen. Yet how many of us live our lives with integrity, sincerity, determination, fortitude, tenderness, grace, generosity? Most of us are quiet stars, shining brightly and beautifully in our own corner of the world, just like the spider I noticed that day, gleaming in stunning beauty in a daylily blossom.

i find myself wondering . . .

Using external mirrors to judge ourselves tends
to reflect back to us only what is superficial.
How can we peer into the blossom of our actual
self, to see the gold within?

take a few moments to reflect . . .

*What parts of yourself do you think are
beautiful? Consider your interior self,
not your exterior image.*

*What parts do you think others see and
respond to?*

*What do you hope people see when they look at/
interact with you?*

*Consider the possibility that on any given day,
you just might be the beautiful thing someone
needs to see.*

3

a patch of moss
noticing small things

While kneeling on the ground this morning to weed out some chickweed and bittercress, I noticed a little patch of moss. The deep green, mounded clump looked like it had a sort of fluffy, bright green top to it. I leaned in for a closer look. The light green fluffiness was a myriad of tiny spore stems, reaching up into the damp spring air. They looked like miniature periscopes, almost as if the moss was trying to see what was above and beyond it.

It's mid-April and there are plenty of other things happening in the plant world that are more eye-catching than sporing moss. The magnolias are in full, fragrant bloom and the slender branches of the redbud trees are clustered with magenta buds just about to open. Daffodils in sunny arrays of yellow and orange are splashed about the yard and the deep, intoxicating aroma of hyacinths comes to my nose on the warm breeze.

Birds flock to the feeders throughout the day. There are flashy red cardinals, iridescent male bluebirds, and bright male goldfinches with their brilliant yellow plumage restored for the spring mating season. Dapper chickadees, nuthatches, and downy woodpeckers vie for seeds and suet as well. Less brightly colored birds also come in abundance; cowbirds, chipping sparrows, grackles, mourning doves, and others are also "regulars." There are robins everywhere.

The mornings are filled with a chorus of birdsong, the evenings with spring peepers who are also making their voices heard as they call out for mates. The grass is greening. New shoots coming up tell me that the perennials have survived, and I know that soon this year's new butterflies will emerge from their cocoons to feed on the flowers' nectar.

In spring, life bursts open—we can't help but notice. But this great transformation counts on more than just the big, flashy changes. Spring also happens in something as small and insignificant as a patch of moss.

There are some signs of life and growth that are so tiny that they rarely, if ever, catch our attention. There are things going on "right beneath our noses," as the apt saying goes, that we simply don't see. And yet these things happening in miniature, unseen, are every bit as important as the big things we do see. They're often just as beautiful.

i find myself wondering . . .

Is it possible that personal transformation also comes in more than big events? Might we have to "lean in" enough to our lives to be able to see the small, but important growth?

take a few moments to reflect . . .

For one month, keep a list of everything that could be considered an accomplishment. Even something as small as remembering to send a birthday card. Or having the confidence to speak up at a meeting.

At the end of the month, read over your list. Can you see your growth?

4

tomato plants
reaching for your goals

In the world today there are over 10,000 kinds of tomatoes. These are separated into categories such as beefsteak, paste, cherry, and grape. And they come in a myriad of colors, from red, green, orange, yellow, and striped, to purple and almost black. There are heirloom varieties, hybrids, and open-pollinated species. Yet, in that whole big world of tomatoes there are just two basic types, known as "determinate" and "indeterminate."

Determinate tomato plants are like trees: they top out at a specific height. Indeterminate varieties keep on growing, clambering up and over anything they can latch onto. If not pruned back, their rampant growth will continue until freezing weather arrives and kills the vines.

This characteristic doesn't in any way influence the flavor of the fruits. It's just useful information for the vegetable grower. But it got me wondering: might people fall into similar categories?

Take me, for instance. If I were a tomato, which type would I be? I like to think that I would be classified as an indeterminate variety, full of the spirit of adventure. In some ways that's true, but practically speaking, I'm much more determinate. Despite a love of adventure and travel, I'm actually a homebody. Determinateness shows up even more in my work. I tend to reach a point where I run out of forward momentum. I reach a pretty good place—a place that could even be labeled "success"— and don't have the energy or interest to go further. Although I might and often do have good ideas for taking something beyond, I just can't seem to get motivated to put in more effort.

Is this the difference between super achievers—those who really push for greatness—and those who don't make that heroic effort? Is my determinate nature set in stone, simply part of my temperament and makeup? If I wanted something badly enough, could I go further? Or do the super achievers of the world have some sort of indeterminate nature that keeps pushing them onward?

I wonder, does it matter? Or is this simply another situation where I might compare myself to others and come up short? I stated earlier that tomatoes taste delicious, regardless of the type of plant that produces them. There's an illusion that we humans are all alike, but of course we're unique beings. We each grow and succeed in our own way.

i find myself wondering . . .

Aren't we essentially all a combination of "determinate" and "indeterminate," limited only by our thoughts, goals, and what we decide we want to achieve?

take a few moments to reflect . . .

Who or what sets the upper limit on a dream or a goal? Is it even possible to know what the upper limit might be? Do we just need to keep exploring?

What's a project you started, where you felt it expanding the farther into it you went?

How would it have been different if you had stopped at your original goal?

5

the fox i didn't see

keeping our eyes open

It was my husband who snagged the photo of the fox as it trotted through our backyard. I was in my study working on this book and had to be satisfied with the photo and with the paw prints the fox left behind in the fresh snow.

It's been like that on so many mornings: Charlie sees the fox; I don't. In fact, I've started thinking of it as "Charlie's fox." After all, my husband is the one who first spotted it and he often reports to me when I finally come downstairs, excitement in his voice, "I saw the fox!" Whereas, in three months or so, I've only seen it once.

Happily, thanks to Charlie, I've got the photo image from that snowy February morning, evidence of this beautiful wild creature that seems to have our property on its morning route. Even so, it's hard not to feel regret at continually missing out on this experience.

Yet, if I were in the kitchen waiting for a possible sighting, I wouldn't have the five hundred words that I'm committed to writing every day before breakfast. And who's to say that I'd see the fox anyway? The viewing opportunity is maybe half a minute. I could sit and wait and still manage to miss it. And then I'd be upset with myself for missing my writing goal.

Truthfully, I can't be too disappointed, because throughout my life I've seen so many amazing and beautiful things. A pair of bald eagles swooping in to perch on a branch so close that I could see every detail of feather and talon. Dozens of tiny, newly hatched snapping turtles spilling out of their nest. A great gyre of thousands of chattering chimney swifts circling down to their roost in the deepening blue twilight.

To see a humpback whale breach—that would be something! But so is seeing a trio of bluebirds at the feeder on a bleak winter's day. To stand under the shimmering, shifting curtain of the northern lights— that would be spine-tingling! But honestly, so is watching the sun set and the stars emerge. Do I need to see every wonderful thing that happens? I think the point is to keep our eyes open. To truly see what is right in front of us. Having a sense of exploration and wonder can turn "ordinary" events into experiences enough to delight us for a lifetime.

i find myself wondering . . .

How much is it possible to see when we keep our eyes open to what is right in front of us?

take a few moments to reflect . . .

What is something you've seen in the natural world that's taken your breath away?

What is something small and "insignificant" that captured your heart and your imagination or stretched the boundaries of your awareness?

How might it change you to notice one small thing each day? To make this a goal?

6

hickory nuts
letting things go

Last week, my husband Charlie and I started Phase
Two of a small landscaping project. There was just one
thing in the way: a three- by four-foot slab of concrete
outside of the back door to the garage that had tipped
up and needed to be leveled. We decided to see if
we could dig out a space beneath it and get it to tilt
back down.

We expected hard-packed, heavy clay and we found it.
What we didn't expect was a chipmunk burrow, stuffed
full of hickory nuts and dead leaves. There was another
surprise: encouraged by rain and warm temperatures,
the nuts had sprouted. In the dark, they had sent up
pale, ghostly stems that were already four or so inches
tall, shoots that would never see the light of day.

It struck me how industrious chipmunks are—and
how much more organized than squirrels, who bury
nuts at random and then forget where they hid them.

By contrast, if not for Charlie and me demolishing the burrow, the chipmunks would know right where to go to find their stash.

Several days later, I found myself thinking about the seeds themselves and what an unfortunate waste it was, their sprouting with no hope of reaching their potential. Was it all for nothing? In the case of the hickory nuts, probably.

But then I realized that it didn't matter. Yes, it was a little sad to think of that wasted effort. But trees "have an app for that." They and other flowering plants produce far more seeds each season than will ever grow to maturity. Think, for instance, of the thousands of maple keys that come spinning down each spring; a maple tree forest doesn't grow up from them. Just as in Jesus' parable of the sower, many of the seeds will fall on pavement or hard ground and won't germinate at all. Many will sprout but not survive. Many will be eaten by wildlife. What's important is that at least some of them take root and grow.

In today's culture, a lot of emphasis is put on following your passion, homing in on that one thing you most want to do in the world, finding and pursuing your "why." But what if that doesn't pan out? Not all of our attempts are going to pay off, no matter how passionate we are about them.

i find myself wondering . . .

It's easy to look at high achievers and believe that their success came from focusing on just one thing. But how many "seeds" did those people plant before that successful one took root?

take a few moments to reflect . . .

What are some things you tried your hand at that didn't work out?

Are you sorry that they didn't pan out?

Did any of those "failures" help lead to your current success?

Is it possible that all of this was perfect?

7

are we there yet?

approaching the summit

‹‹‹‹‹

Finally, there it was—the summit! We'd been hiking up (and up!) for nearly two hours. Yes, the scenery was beautiful. And yes, I was enjoying almost every step of the way. But now that I could see the top of the mountain, I realized how happy I was that we were finally about to reach our goal. There was still some serious climbing to do, but this milestone was now within reach.

Except that it wasn't. When we arrived at what we thought was the end, we saw that the trail took a turn to the right and down, back into scrub forest, with no sign of the actual mountaintop in view from where we now stood.

What a surprise and disappointment to reach this point, only to discover that it was a false summit and there was obviously farther to go. Pausing in silent agreement, we shrugged off our packs and enjoyed a few sips of water before moving on again. About thirty minutes and another false summit later, we found ourselves standing happily on the actual top, with a marker to prove it.

When we started out on this hike, we thought we knew the way, but we didn't really. We knew, of course, that we'd be climbing "up," and we knew the height of the mountain, but beyond that we had no idea of how many twists and turns the trail would take, or how many times it would lead us up only to drop us down again into a hollow.

Over the years, this trail has become a favorite of ours and we've returned to it many times. It's a wonderfully satisfying hike, with great views at various points along the way. Did we get discouraged that first time, when we realized that we weren't on the top of the mountain yet? A little bit, sure. But we knew that we were on the right path. And we knew that we were always getting closer. Both those things kept us going.

Climbing a mountain is a familiar metaphor for life, and for good reason. Life takes determination, especially if we want to do more than just exist. With almost anything we set our sights on, there can be many twists and turns, and innumerable high and low points. If we want to reach a goal, it's important to have a clear sense of our vision.

i find myself wondering . . .

In life, achieving one goal often leads to another. And another. Often there isn't a clearly-defined "summit." So, how do we decide when we've reached "the top?" Maybe we can use these not-quite-there places to take a breath, enjoy the scenery, and contemplate if there's a further destination we want to reach.

take a few moments to reflect . . .

What's a big goal that you went after and reached?

Did you get there in one straight shot, or were there false summits along the way?

Do you enjoy being able to see yet another goal above you?

When and how do you decide that you've reached the top?

8

barefoot in the garden

staying grounded

For all the time that I spent running around barefoot as a child, it wasn't until I was well into adulthood that I realized just how much I love having my feet on the ground, walking with no shoes or sandals between my own human skin and the skin of the earth. There's an aliveness, a sensuousness, an immediacy that I revel in. I even have a practice of walking barefoot to the compost bin each day until winter approaches and the temperature drops close to freezing.

I could describe this as being something like the difference between holding someone's gloved hand or being skin-to-skin. And yet I can't quite grasp or express what it is, really, about going barefoot. It's more than the freedom of having my feet unconfined, more than the tactile sensation of walking across a lush, grassy lawn or a nearly frozen one. In an experience that is so tangible, there's something that I find surprisingly elusive.

As I continue to explore this, I realize that the places my bare feet love the most and feel the most deeply connected are the smooth, bare-earth paths between the rows of vegetables in my garden. I know that I should put down mulch to help keep weeds at bay, but I just can't bring myself to do it. I would miss that vital, sustaining bit of communion between the ground of my being—my physical self—and the earth. We humans are, after all, made of the same elements contained in the earth.

Doesn't all life—whether human, animal, or vegetable—ultimately spring from the ground? We have only to consider all of the plants from which we get our food and the materials for our shelter, the plants that feed the animals that some of us consume. Ultimately, as I've heard it said, civilization comes down to "twelve inches of topsoil and the fact that it rains." We are intricately bound up with the very substance of the earth, so why shouldn't we feel a strong, intimate connection with it?

Over thousands of years, we humans have worked to better protect ourselves with clothing and shelter, making a sort of second skin between us and the environment. And that's paid off for us. Safe from weather, wild animals, and poisonous insects, we're free to create, to relax, to simply be. Today, we could probably spend an entire lifetime without going outside. But have we lost something along the way?

i find myself wondering . . .

There's no question that with all of our
protections, we're safer. And yet we yearn,
don't we, for connection with something
elemental, something that grounds us physically
to our sense of being?

take a few moments to reflect . . .

What are some ways that you stay grounded?
Is it walking barefoot? Swimming in the ocean?
Tending a potted plant? Something else?

Do you find deep connection in other tactile
pursuits, e.g., sewing or painting?

Could you also simply breathe in the air and
know you're breathing it?

9

the sentience of trees
being connected

From the time I was young, I felt a kinship with trees. I felt that trees were my friends, and I spent a lot of time with them. I climbed in them. Built forts in them. Hugged them.

A picnic area in a grove of towering white pine trees at a local state park was a favorite spot. There seemed to be a sort of magical aliveness there. But even as a little girl I knew that I wanted to see and spend some time with Really Big Trees. Old trees. So, it was an amazing experience as a teenager to stumble upon Jenkins Woods, a 125-acre preserve of old-growth hemlock forest in northeastern Pennsylvania.

Sadly, none of the old giants were still standing; they remained only in great fallen trunks and decaying stumps. But the woods had the *feeling* of "ancient." A deep, spongy layer representing countless years of fallen needles and humus cushioned my steps.

Mosses and ferns were everywhere. And it was so incredibly quiet.

A trip to the Hoh Rainforest in Washington and a drive through a California redwood forest many years later gave me the ultimate Big Tree experience I'd been wishing for. As I wandered among the giant trunks, looking up and up and up, I sensed the aliveness and strength of the trees.

Recent research now shows that what I sensed is true: trees are alive in ways that we never knew before. They may look inert, but in fact they are continuously engaged with each other. Trees being attacked by insects can send out a warning to their neighbors. "Mother trees" share nutrients with both their own offspring and with other species. They do this underground, with the help of a certain type of fungi called mycorrhizae. These fungi create vast networks that connect root tips to root tips.

Trees don't grow near each other just because that's where their seeds fall. They grow in communities because they are stronger that way.

In learning this about trees, I recall the times I've needed to borrow something from a neighbor. Times I've given someone a ride when their car is in the shop. Times I've made meals for a friend going through chemo. I've seen neighborhoods raise funds to help pay medical costs for a struggling family. Like trees, we humans are stronger in community, too.

i find myself wondering . . .

> With just a computer click or two we can now learn about and send aid to others in need that we've never even met. Just like trees, doesn't this help us build community?

take a few moments to reflect . . .

> *Think of a time when you asked a friend or neighbor for help or when someone asked you for help.*
>
> *Did you feel stronger through this connection, even if was just borrowing a newspaper?*
>
> *Did sharing in this way help you feel like part of a community?*
>
> *What about when you've helped someone you haven't even met?*

10

the star in an apple
changing perspective

I don't remember when I first saw the star inside
an apple. It may have been in college, in my plant
taxonomy class, as we learned how to distinguish
the ways that botanists organize plants into different
families. Or it might have been the day my young son
cut an apple the "wrong" way—around the middle—
rather than from top to bottom. It doesn't really matter
when this happened. The point is that a star had been
hiding in every apple I'd ever eaten; I just never knew it.
And, not knowing, I'd never seen it.

What I loved, equally as much as discovering that
hidden star, was the realization that simply by
repositioning an apple on the cutting board, I could
find something so beautiful and so surprising inside.
Even though it's easier to cut apples top to bottom to
remove the seeds, I still sometimes will cut around the
"equator" just to glimpse that simple, perfect little star.

To botanists, the star pattern speaks of the Rose Family, easily identified by plant parts in groups of five: five petals, five sepals, five seed chambers. To me, the five-pointed star speaks past science to art and beauty; there is just something so perfect and awe-inspiring about this arrangement and how deliberate it is. Not to mention that while it's a challenge for me to draw a perfect five-pointed star, nature seems to have no problem with this pattern or with others that are far more complex.

Cutting along a different line and finding order and beauty that I didn't see before shows me that beauty and delight can be all around us without our seeing it. That is, until we find ourselves, or put ourselves, at a different perspective.

Reminders of this happen constantly. For example, my husband will call out, "Look! There's a hawk in the tree!" I look toward where he's pointing, but I don't see the hawk—not until I change my position so that there are no branches blocking my line of sight. The bird was there, but I couldn't see it until I moved.

i find myself wondering . . .

Is it possible that many of the things we think we know and believe as fact might change if we could get a different perspective on them?

take a few moments to reflect . . .

Can you think of a time when you felt you were right, only to discover that your "line of sight" was limited?

Can remembering such a time help you feel less aggravated with other people, when they just don't seem to "get" something that you think is so obvious?

How might you change or expand your view?

11

empty spaces

making room

Looking out the kitchen window as I wash up the breakfast dishes, I can see the old pin oak tree in the backyard. Reaching about sixty feet toward the sky it still stands straight, though many of its limbs are dead or dying. From my vantage point, I can see the rounded holes in the upper branches and tapering trunk where hungry woodpeckers have tapped into the decaying wood, digging for insects.

Recently, a rotted branch that could no longer support even its much lighter decayed weight dropped to the ground. Kneeling next to it, I inspected the large, circular holes, so perfectly shaped. I wondered at how something as massive and dense as an oak tree can be dismantled by things as tiny as burrowing insects and bird beaks.

The process is normal. Expected. Trees age, rot, and provide fodder for insects, which provide food for birds. So, what is there to wonder about this empty space other than to be curious if small birds might decide to nest in such a spot? And yet I do wonder beyond the obvious. The wood that was once there—where is it now? What is an empty space, really? Other places we see as empty—were they also once filled with something?

I think about places in myself that feel empty. The places where friendships used to be before friends drifted away. The place that was occupied by running before my back started to protest. The place where I cared for my son before he became an adult. This seems to be how life works: either by choice or by fate something is in our life until it isn't. This winnowing away, this creation of empty spots, is just part of the process.

Of course, "empty" typically doesn't feel good. But maybe we're supposed to have these unfilled spots. There certainly isn't enough time and space for absolutely everything we want. Maybe a bit of winnowing is what we need. And maybe that new space will be an invitation to something else. Empty can also mean opportunity.

Our intricate English language isn't always precise. For instance, what does empty really mean? I remember seeing an example of someone tossing a lighted match into an empty barrel. Volatile fumes still present from the chemical previously stored in the barrel caught fire. Obviously, the container wasn't actually empty. At the very least, volatiles aside, an "empty" barrel contains air.

i find myself wondering . . .

Is it possible that when we lose something—a job, a relationship, a friend—it's the universe's "woodpecker," chipping away at things that no longer serve, making space for something else?

take a few moments to reflect . . .

Is there an empty place that you've been feeling within yourself? Can you identify it?

Is there still something there, like the volatile vapor in the barrel?

Can you accept that what used to occupy that space is truly gone?

Can you let it simply fall away?

12

redbud trees
seeding dreams

When we first moved to our house here in southeastern Pennsylvania, I planted a redbud tree near the driveway. That way, I could see the tree every time I drove in or out. What I didn't anticipate is that we would eventually have dozens of these lovely little trees everywhere around the property.

Native to the eastern U.S., the eastern redbud (*Cercis canadensis*) is a tree that isn't particularly fussy about where it grows—it thrives whether it's in sun or shade, loam, or clay—or how much water it gets. It only grows to about twenty feet or so, making it perfect for small yards or naturalized borders. All that would be enough, but redbuds are spectacular in early spring when clusters of rose-purple flowers bloom profusely on bare branches. It's like having a *corps de ballet* in pink tutus positioned all around the yard.

What's surprising is that I only ever planted that one tree. For the others, I credit squirrels, birds, and deer that must have dropped partially eaten seed pods at random.

Every spring, I pull out dozens of new seedlings that crop up in the flower beds. I know that these are only a small fraction of what there would be if every seed took root. Like any plant that produces seeds, a redbud makes way more than will ever grow, because only a small percentage of them will germinate, take root, and survive to maturity. Some seeds will be eaten by wildlife. Some won't get enough water. Some will simply be "outcompeted" and won't get enough sunlight or nutrients. If a tree relied on just one seed to replicate itself, we'd never have a sustainable forest

I look at the redbuds and remember nature walks in springtime with my dad; how many times he'd pick up a maple key (a.k.a., samara) and say, "Look how prolific nature is! One tree makes all these seeds so that at least a few will survive to become new trees." Because a tree can't plant and tend its own seeds, it relies on numbers and some good fortune to get the job done.

An idea that's been popularized over the last ten years or so is that you should figure out what your passion is and then devote yourself to that one thing, not letting anything stand in your way. It's certainly important to devote yourself to a goal, but, as the redbud demonstrates, I think there's also wisdom in not putting all your eggs in one basket.

i find myself wondering . . .

Things don't always work out, no matter how much we want them to or how much effort we put into them. Besides that, who says we can't have more than one dream?

take a few moments to reflect . . .

Do you find it challenging to settle on just the One Thing to do with your life?

List all the things that call to you, large and small.

Consider your list: are there compatible goals, ones that you could combine into one career?

How can you nourish all of these?

13

a lesson from a caterpillar

creating a support system

It was late at night and the house was asleep, except for me and the black swallowtail caterpillar in the habitat I'd set up for it in an old aquarium. Looking over from my snug spot on the sofa, I noticed that the caterpillar, which had been immobile since earlier in the day, was still in the same spot but was now moving, arching its head back and forth. I got up to see what was happening and discovered that I'd managed to catch the caterpillar in the act of making the sling from which it would later hang as a chrysalis.

A black swallowtail doesn't go directly from larva to pupa. Before that transformation, the caterpillar makes itself a little harness that it attaches to the surface of a carefully chosen spot. That's what I was now witnessing in the near-dark living room. The larva moved its upper body back and forth, from left to right and back again, spinning out barely visible silken threads from its spinnerets. I watched as it laid down dozens of these threads, making an almost impossibly thin strand. After several minutes of this, the larva began to stretch the fine cable and then worked its head and upper body under the sling until the loop was wrapped around its back. Finally, it settled in and was still again. No more movement.

Two nights later, after hours of constant watching and waiting, I got to witness the caterpillar split out of its skin, revealing the chrysalis beneath. Through the entire bizarre process, which takes only eight minutes or so, the sling remained intact. The chrysalis will remain suspended by the sling through the winter and early spring, until it emerges as a butterfly sometime next May.

I was blown away by this. And it got me thinking. In all the attention that's placed on the transformation of caterpillars to butterflies—using that as a metaphor for personal transformation, and how challenging and sometimes painful transformation can be—I've never heard anyone mention what happens *before*, i.e., that the larva makes a supportive sling for itself.

As I thought about this, I wondered: in the really rough times in our lives, what is *our* support? What holds us fast as we struggle and morph, and morph again, and finally break out of our old "skin?" I realized that for me, it starts with family, friends, my version of prayer. It then goes beyond—to playing music, writing, being in nature.

i find myself wondering . . .

Is a support system something that we instinctively create for ourselves? Are there invisible supports we create that we're not even aware of—practices, habits, rituals?

take a few moments to reflect . . .

Who or what holds you when you feel immobilized by life—by anxiety, loss, grief, traumatic change?

If you haven't felt support when you needed it, how can you create it so it's there when you do?

With support in place, can you relax into trust and let your life unfold?

14

the old oak tree

aging with grace

This morning I stood at my kitchen sink, rinsing the mug that I use for my breakfast tea. At just eight degrees Fahrenheit, it's the coldest day of the year so far. A north wind is sweeping the brittle air through the branches of the trees so that the landscape looks like it's dancing. But not the old pin oak. That one tree looks like an elderly person at the edge of a dance floor, clutching a walker and stiffly shuffling to the music.

When this tree was still in its middle age, I'd watch the birds flying in and out of the lofty, leaf-covered branches. I reveled in the delicious shade that helped make hot, humid summers easier to bear. Long life is a trait of oaks, and I expected—hoped—that this tree would live more or less forever.

My expectation did not play out. The oak contracted an untreatable condition common to this particular species. The arborist said there was nothing to be done.

And so, over the past fifteen years I've watched the tree fall apart. The strong, furrowed bark has ripped open. Many of the beautiful, graceful "arms" have broken off mid-branch and dropped to the ground below. The rotted limbs weigh almost nothing, and I easily drag them aside. It's my heart that's heavy.

Surprisingly, though, my sadness has turned into appreciation and gratitude. Because that tree is helping me. With fewer large branches and with so much less foliage, it's no longer the wonderful neighborhood it used to be for birds and squirrels. And yet, it's really only the demographics that have changed. Multiple large holes in the upper branches are evidence of woodpeckers searching for insects in the rotted wood. These holes provide nesting habitat.

I love that the tree and I are growing old together and that the tree has so much to tell me about the process. It can't do all the things that it used to do and neither can I. The tree is still itself and yet it's different. As it changes, it's finding different ways to be in the world, different ways to be useful. Like me.

As we go through different stages of life, we often find ourselves naturally shedding some of the things we used to do, just as that oak tree has shed its biggest, heaviest branches. I can now see that this opens up new possibilities, opportunities that wouldn't have been obvious to us or might even have been impossible for us when we were younger.

i find myself wondering . . .

Where did we ever get the idea that after you retire, your job as an elder is simply to be old? Why can't stepping into old age bring a whole new career, full of possibility?

take a few moments to reflect . . .

Think back over your life so far.

What are some things that you've grown out of? What are some of your newer activities? What do you still look forward to accomplishing?

Can you see that your whole life has been a process of "shedding" and moving into new activities and endeavors?

15

the mud dauber wasp

being persistent

It was fixing to be another hot, steamy July day, so I
went out early to pick some vegetables for dinner. Out
of the corner of my eye I noticed something on a small,
bare patch of earth in the lawn near the garden. It was
a black-and-yellow-striped wasp, moving around on the
dry, dusty patch. I was curious. Why would a wasp be on
the ground? Shouldn't it be flying around or feeding on
something?

I crouched down for a better look. Now I could see
that the wasp was moving its front legs in a repetitive
motion. As I watched, I saw that it was rolling up a tiny
ball of earth. Suddenly, the wasp flew off, carrying the
little ball with it.

After bringing my basket of cucumbers, tomatoes, and
zucchini into the kitchen, I went back outside to the
place where I had seen the wasp. It was there again,
busily working on gathering another minuscule ball of

earth. This time I watched and followed to see where the wasp went. It landed on the front of the house, near the door. There, on the bricks—scarcely visible unless you looked for it—was a tiny clay nest. I watched as the wasp added its new little ball of mud to it and then flew off, back to that same patch of bare earth. Fascinated, I watched this activity for a long time, sometimes kneeling on the grass to observe the rolling up of the little balls of dirt, sometimes standing by the house, watching the nearly imperceptible additions to the clay structure.

I have no idea how many balls of mud the wasp had to make to build her nest and how many trips she made—I didn't have the time or patience to watch and count—but it must have been hundreds. What a long, tedious job! Yet the wasp continued and eventually created many nests, for all her eggs. In this matter of survival for her young, she persisted until the work was done.

There's no way to know if wasps think about the finished nests while they're building them. They probably work purely by instinct. We humans, though, can keep a goal in mind through all the myriad, sometimes frustrating steps involved—whether it's for a wedding, a job hunt, training for a marathon, or doing a home remodeling project. Imagining the end result keeps us going.

i find myself wondering . . .

There's a big difference between drudgery
and fun, yet maybe it's actually a fine line.
Can changing our attitude toward a project
transform it from a chore to a fun challenge?

take a few moments to reflect . . .

*Think of a project you've worked on that felt
like fun.*

*Think of a project that felt like nothing but
a chore.*

What was the difference?

*What could you have done to make the chore
feel more like fun? More like an opportunity?*

NOTE: The wasp I saw is called a mud dauber wasp. If you'd like to
see one in action, check out this video on YouTube: http://www.
youtube.com/watch?v=BWr66LEqav0. The wasp in the video rolls
up balls of mud from a wet patch of earth. When these wasps can't
find mud, they will mix their saliva with dry earth to make the little
balls of mud, like the wasp that I watched.

See appendix on page 121 for QR code of the website referenced.

16

the walnut shell

doing what we can

Coming up the walk to my front door yesterday, I found an empty half-shell of a black walnut lying on the pavement. Over the years, I've seen hundreds of these nuts, so I could have just ignored it. But I picked up this fragment because I realized that I was looking at something I'd never seen before: the smooth, polished interior of one of these big, rough-looking tree seeds.

A flurry of thoughts flooded my mind. First, I was struck by the beauty and intricacy of the curved, hollow chambers. Second, I wondered how a squirrel—with only its teeth and tiny hands—had managed to remove every speck of the nut from inside that shell. For that matter, how had the squirrel opened the shell in the first place?

Black walnut trees are common in this part of Pennsylvania and each October they drop their big, heavy nuts by the thousands, with many of the fruits falling onto lawns and streets. I know people who eagerly await the annual nutting season, driving here and there to collect the bounty and gathering it up in big plastic buckets. Back at home, the first thing they do is pour the nuts onto their driveway, then crush open the hard, green outer shells by running back and forth over them with their car.

It's only then that the real fun begins. Black walnuts have much thicker shells than English walnuts. For English walnuts, you just need a nutcracker. For black walnuts, you need a hammer, a nut pick, and a really strong "why." Some people resort to crushing the walnuts with a vise grip and then pick out the small, edible bits and pieces from the rubble. Though the nutmeat inside is deliciously sweet, it's a painstaking process to get to it. And the pieces that are left look nothing like the beautiful, mostly intact half-shell I found.

Beyond an uncanny ability to get to the seed in my bird feeders and chasing each other around the yard like kids on a playground, I don't know many things squirrels excel at, but extracting the meat from these tough, complex-chambered nuts seems to be one of them. And it made me stop and think: why can't I do that?

i find myself wondering . . .

Of course, I'm not a squirrel, so it's a silly comparison. But what if we could avoid comparing what we can and can't do with other people the same way we do with other creatures?

take a few moments to reflect . . .

Think of someone you compare yourself to, who has skills or abilities you wish you had.

Does it really matter that you can't do those things?

Now, think of something you're really good at or something you simply enjoy doing. Can you fully appreciate that?

stuck on a mountainside

creating a buffer

The summer air was clear, the sun was bright, and my friend Sally and I were hiking the Dudley Trail up the north side of Mount Katahdin in Maine. We'd applied for a hiking and camping reservation a year before and were elated to finally be here.

Katahdin, the northern end of the Appalachian Trail, is sort of the holy grail of hiking in the eastern United States. Just a few feet shy of a mile high, it's not a tall prospect, especially compared to Denali and the other great western peaks. But Katahdin has this thing called the Knife Edge, a 1.1-mile narrow, rocky trail that traverses the rim of an ancient glacial cirque. If you miss your footing, you risk a drop of 2,000 feet on either side and that's a lot, regardless of a mountain's total height. People do fall here. Some die.

We weren't planning to attempt the Knife Edge, but I didn't expect that climbing up to it to take a look would feel so treacherous. The upper part of the trail turned out to be a great boulder field, pitched so steeply that I felt that the weight of my small pack might tip me over backwards. There is no trail here, only a general indication of "up," leaving hikers to clamber over and around the boulders as they wish.

I was doing pretty well until I reached a place where I was unable to find another hand or toehold to move forward. Going back down seemed even more impossible. In that instant of feeling stuck, panic set in: how was I going to get off the mountain? Obviously, I eventually managed to calm myself enough to find some handholds and start moving upward again. But it was a bad ten minutes or so and it took me a while to stop shaking.

Several years later, I went trekking in the Himalayas. Contrary to the assurances from the tour company that I'd be fine, there were plenty of scary spots. Curiously, the worst place—with a drop as treacherous as any on Katahdin—didn't spook me at all. The reason? There was a little fringe of vegetation growing along the outer edge of the trail that buffered my view of the empty space below. I realized that if I don't *see* the danger of falling, I don't feel it.

i find myself wondering . . .

If not seeing danger can keep fear at bay, what is it that we're really afraid of?

take a few moments to reflect . . .

Have you ever avoided doing something because it seemed too scary?

What would you do if you weren't afraid?

What's a "fringe" that you could create for yourself?

18

spiders in the window
finding a niche

Cellar spiders. Despite the name, these arachnids and their webs are often found elsewhere about the house—across ceilings, in corners, behind doors. With their small bodies and ultra-thin, segmented legs, they're easily mistaken for daddy longlegs. They eat insects and even consume other spiders, so I leave them alone until the cobwebs have proliferated and start to look untidy—creepy, even—with their dark, dusty strands.

Last summer I discovered that two baby cellar spiders had set up shop at the window over the kitchen sink, in the space between the glass and the screen. We almost always keep that window closed so I wondered how the spiders would survive in there. How would they get food? I thought that they needed an open foraging area and that the window was a death-trap. I was wrong.

Over the next several weeks, I watched as the spiders continued to remain alive. Bit by bit, they grew from tiny, frail-looking things to larger, not-quite-as-frail things. But what were they eating? When I looked closely, I could see tiny, tell-tale "crumbs" beneath the little webs. These were obviously the remains of prey, bundled up in wrappings of spider silk, sucked dry, and eventually dropped from the web. Perhaps they had been fruit flies; I couldn't tell. What was important was the fact that the insects were small enough to get through the fine mesh of the window screen.

That's when I realized the flaws in my interpretation of the spiders' location: my own sense of what a life should be, my own idea of the importance of freedom and what freedom actually is. For most creatures, their life's work is to survive long enough to spawn new life. Eventually, every creature dies, living on only in the progeny it's managed to procreate. In their limited space, the spiders had found a niche to accomplish that. Who was I to think they needed more?

I started thinking about what's really necessary for a rich, nourishing, satisfying life. I'm a writer, a newspaper columnist, and a musician. Do I need to move to New York City for the best opportunities? The skills that are enough for me to be principal cellist in a local chamber orchestra probably wouldn't earn me last chair in a big-city group. Columnist gigs are hard to come by and

I wouldn't be assured of finding a new one if I tried to start over. I realized that I have all the nourishment I need right where I am.

i find myself wondering . . .

> Is a seemingly too-small environment really a limitation? Can we do better or just as well in life by maximizing the opportunities where we are, rather than wishing or striving to be somewhere else?

take a few moments to reflect . . .

> *Consider your situation. Are you able to pursue and maximize your interests where you are?*
>
> *What would you gain by moving somewhere else?*
>
> *What would you lose?*

19

the story of a seed

setting intentions

In 2005, the legendary Judean date palm, extinct since about 500 A.D., was resurrected when Israeli botanist Elaine Solowey managed to get a roughly 2,000-year-old seed to germinate. The tree, which is still going strong, was dubbed "Methuselah," after the oldest person in the Bible. I was so fascinated by the story that I decided to try and sprout a fresh date seed; I wanted to see if I could do it and how long it would take.

Solowey had soaked a batch of ancient seeds in a nutrient/enzyme solution. It took months, but eventually she saw a sign of life—a tiny crack that opened up in one of them. I treated a fresh seed—saved from a date I bought at the grocery store—to a mere 48-hour soak in plain water and then to a stay in the refrigerator, tucked within the folds of a damp paper towel and sealed inside a plastic Ziplock™ bag. In just two weeks the hard shell softened, cracked opened, and a root emerged. A month or so later, a tiny palm frond poked out: success!

And now I have a dilemma.

Here's my problem. I'm not that interested in having a palm tree for a house plant and I don't live in a climate where a palm tree can stay outside year-round. What should I do with it? Should I toss it outside now, while it's still small? Should I let it grow indoors until it gets too big—and *then* heave it onto the compost pile? Should I continue to tend the tree, inside, for the rest of its life?

You may be wondering why this is a question at all. I mean, it's just a plant, right? My quandary is that I feel responsible; after all, I called this little seedling into life. Of course, I can rationalize and say, "It was just an experiment." One could even argue that deliberately letting a tiny tree die is not a terrible offense. Is it really any different from planting annuals in my garden, knowing full well that they won't survive the winter?

Beyond this botanical moral dilemma, the question of what to do with the date-palm seedling started me thinking about how we begin new projects. Specifically, do we think them through before starting? Do we stop to consider how invested we are in seeing them completed? What if we run into stumbling blocks? What projects do we push on with, regardless? Which do we let lapse?

i find myself wondering . . .

Is it possible that some failures are not the result of something we failed to do during the life of a project, but something we failed to do before we started?

take a few moments to reflect . . .

Call a project to mind, one that was your "baby" and that you completed.

Call a project to mind, one that was your "baby" that you didn't complete or follow through on or give your all.

What contributed to your completion of the one project? What led to the abandonment of the other?

Update: The scientists continued to germinate other ancient Judean date palm seeds, hoping to generate a viable female tree and reproduce actual fruits. Success came in 2020. You can read about it here: https://nocamels.com/2020/09/2000-ancient-judean-dates-israeli-scientists/

See appendix on page 121 for QR code of the website referenced.

20

the gift of rain

making the most of the day

It's raining—an almost perfect rain, coming down
in a steady but light patter. I hear the nuances of it,
the differences in sound depending on whether the
drops land on leaves, lawn, pavement, or roof, yet all
blending into one lovely voice. This rain-music makes a
companionable backdrop to the day.

Because of the rain, I won't be going outside today.
Won't be gardening. Will forego my usual walk. So many
things I'll be missing, yet I couldn't be happier.

In this, I seem to be going against the norm. More and
more, lately, I've seen TV weather reporters apologizing
for even just a single day of rain, as if to say that
anything but blue skies, 80-degree temperatures, and
low humidity is an insult. What has happened to us?
Have we become so detached from our environment
that we can't recognize that we need rainy weather as
well as dry?

Sure, too many days of pounding rain can be oppressive. But I've lived through weeks and months when it didn't rain, and that wore on my psyche equally as much. Plus, a rainy day or two means that I don't have to water the garden and container plants. A rainy day washes pollen out of the air and gives the car a bath.

It may be my introverted nature talking, but I appreciate days when I don't feel called to be outside *doing*. I put a high value on time to tuck in, putter around the house, read, perhaps enjoy a nap. In my family, we even have a name for it. We call such an opportunity a "snack-n-snooze" day and we enjoy it for all it's worth. And there are other benefits.

A journal entry from our 2019 Maine vacation helps tell the story:

"After a stretch of beautiful, sunny days, we woke up today to rain. There will be no hiking or swimming. It's chilly, so we won't even be lounging/reading on the porch. It's a little sad. But it's actually lovely to have a weather-enforced "snack-n-snooze" day while we're on vacation."

There's a little more to it. My journal entry continues: *"The thing that makes it a blessing instead of a curse is that we've been hiking and swimming the whole time, as many days as possible."* I love the balance this implies and what I've learned: take advantage of what each day has to offer, and there will be nothing to regret, only to enjoy.

i find myself wondering . . .

> Why do we spend so much time complaining about the weather? One person is glad that it's raining, not snowing, but the skier is disappointed. Can we learn to enjoy what we have?

take a few moments to reflect . . .

> *Do you chafe when "bad" weather keeps you inside?*
>
> *Do you waste time feeling angry about it, when you could be doing something else?*
>
> *What about putting together a "rainy-day" kit, with a book you've been meaning to read, a sewing or art project, some nice stationery and pen, or a rainy-day journal?*

21

the promise of seeds

growing where you're planted

Several years ago, my next-door neighbor planted a bed of asparagus. If you're familiar with growing this edible perennial, you know that the project took a lot of work. After figuring out the best site, Tom double-dug a trench two feet deep and about a foot wide along an eight-foot length—no mean feat in the heavy, rock-strewn clay that's typical of this area. Then he backfilled the trench, mixing in lots of compost. Then he planted the asparagus crowns. And then he waited the recommended two years before harvesting more than a test stalk or two, to give the plants time to get fully established.

Last year Tom finally got a harvest. And this year I got a surprise: two bright-green, five-inch, needle-leaved stalks growing under the arborvitae hedge and a third one growing under the oak tree. I'd never seen anything like them before. What were they? I tried to imagine that these were offspring of the arborvitae trees or of the red cedar growing near the oak. But no; the leaves of these little seedlings were too soft and feathery for conifers. My moment of bewilderment vanished as I realized that I was looking at baby asparagus plants. Birds must have gone after the berries on my neighbor's plants last fall and left some seeds in their droppings here and there on my property. These plants may not thrive where they are—the random, current location may not provide an optimum growing environment—but my first thought was, "So much for all that double-digging!"

This spring I also noticed an echinacea plant growing up in the seam where the driveway meets the garage. It obviously seeded in from one of the plants in the flower bed in front of the house, it obviously gets enough water through that bit of an opening, and it must have enough root room. It's strong and healthy and has flower buds just the same as the garden plants. Is this the most convenient place to have a plant? No. But I'm so full of admiration for it that I can't bring myself to pull it out.

Like the asparagus seedlings, nothing told this echinacea that it needed better soil or perfect conditions to take root and grow. It had found everything it needed— water, warmth, a place to be rooted, sunlight, nutrients, *enough*. If it had waited for something better, the seed might not have lasted through a second winter. Why not break out of its shell and see what's possible?

i find myself wondering . . .

Many people achieve success without wealthy parents or a college degree. How much of success is due to environment? How much depends on what we bring to a project, a dream, our lives?

take a few moments to reflect . . .

What determines whether an environment is satisfactory or not? Does it have to be "perfect?"

Can you grow where you are?

If your environment is truly holding you back but you have no options to move, what are ways that you can modify your environment? Do you need more of something? Less of something?

22

the ruby-throated hummingbird

being in the right place

It was *hot*. The unprecedented, early-June heat wave with no rain in sight had me out daily to water the beleaguered plants. On this particular morning I had made the rounds of the vegetable garden and the patio plants and was finishing up with the planting beds in front of the house. Feeling the laziness of the day's heat, I stood in one place, adjusting the hose nozzle so that I could reach the farthest plants without moving. For the last bit of watering, I angled the spray onto a bed of mint about twelve feet from where I was standing.

Suddenly, I saw a small, dark shape take flight out of the foliage. I thought that I must have disturbed a big bumblebee. I diverted the spray, not wanting to disturb any other bees. But as the insect moved toward me, I could see that it was much larger. A dragonfly or cicada wasp maybe? The shape came closer and into the light. And then my jaw literally dropped as an "Ahhhhh!"

escaped my lips. It was a ruby-throated hummingbird, with the sunlight bouncing off its neck. This was a jolt of color I'd never seen before. Somewhere in the back of my mind flashed the thought that this is why they're called "ruby-throated." Because it looked like the tiny bird was wearing a breastplate of actual rubies, infused with the light of the sun so that they appeared to be lit from within. For the first time in my life, I felt my breath taken away.

The little bird came right up to the water of the hose. I adjusted the nozzle to a fine spray and watched as the hummingbird began sipping and bathing in the mist, ducking in and out, over and over again, giving more opportunity for my eyes to try and comprehend that gem-like color. It was dazzling. Mesmerizing. Adding to the magic of the moment was the fact that I hadn't planned it; couldn't have planned it.

We choose many things in our lives—friends, spouse/partner, how we spend our free time, what foods we eat, whether or not we exercise, spending or saving, and even our thoughts. Then, without warning, inexplicable, wonderful, unchosen things fall into our path. We can call it serendipity, grace, a miracle. A fluke, dumb luck, providence. Whatever word we use, the fact remains that we can't actually explain how things like this happen.

I find myself wondering . . .

Planning is necessary, but micro-managing can encourage us to think that we're in control. Do unpredictable events serve to remind us that life also just happens? That unplanned events often chart our course?

take a few moments to reflect . . .

Have you ever had the experience of being "in the right place at the right time?"

Did it affect your life in any way? If yes, how?

How might your life be different if you relaxed your need to be in control and went more with the flow?

NOTE: After this experience, I learned that the neck feathers of the male ruby-throated hummingbird are unpigmented. When light falls on them, the feathers act like tiny prisms, refracting the intense, rosy hue. Without a light source, or if the bird's head is turned, the feathers look dull, sometimes almost black. You really do need to be in the right place at the right time. In my case, I was 68 years old and had seen many hummingbirds before I saw the phenomenon of the ruby throat for the first time.

23

a colony of ants

the art of communicating

As I was walking across the grocery store parking lot the other day, I noticed a gazillion or so ants moving in a long column on the pavement. Some were scurrying in one direction, the rest in the opposite direction. I couldn't help but wonder what they were doing. From my human vantage point, it seemed unlikely that any of them knew where they were going, and yet each seemed intent on a purpose.

Ants are so tiny that unless I find them crawling on me, barging in on a picnic, or invading the kitchen, they're easy to overlook. But just as with any other living creature, if I stop to investigate it's like opening a good novel—there's so much to know and to explore.

I remember the day in third grade when one of my classmates brought in an ant farm for show-and-tell. I can still recall how fascinated I was, watching the ants in a habitat so narrow that I could follow their underground workings.

Seeing the ants within the confines of the habitat it was easy to discern several different roles, as some of the ants carried eggs, some carried food, and others busied themselves in excavating new tunnels. At the time, it didn't occur to me to wonder how each ant knew what to do and how they navigated the confined space without creating traffic jams. But it did occur to me to wonder that day in the parking lot as I watched so many ants on the move. Had they all gotten some kind of internal ant memo?

It finally occurred to me that just because I couldn't see the ants' form of communication, that didn't mean it didn't exist. I mean, if some alien creature were to look down on an Earth community, what would it see? Millions of us humans hurrying about, walking, driving, going to work, to school, to sporting events, church, concerts, or stopping to chat with a neighbor. Without seeing our emails, text messages, phone calls, and newspaper notices, wouldn't our movements seem as inexplicable as the ants' actions seemed to me?

Of course, we communicate a lot without words, too— a gesture or facial expression can express volumes. Crossed arms and a scowl can say, "I'm in a bad mood. Don't bother me!" A blank stare can express boredom. Slumped shoulders may say that we're feeling discouraged. Many times, we're not even aware that we're sending out signals and that people are picking up on them.

I find myself wondering . . .

Despite thousands of years of increasingly sophisticated human communication—letters, newspapers, books, email, TV, videos, the internet—doesn't a lot of our communication still depend on visual cues? Isn't this why someone invented emojis?

take a few moments to reflect . . .

Is it possible that sometimes you're "saying" something you're not aware of?

What might your unspoken signals tell others about you?

Do you think these make a difference in how people relate to you?

24

the view from the hilltop

getting perspective

For over twenty years, my family has spent our annual summer vacation in Maine. The little cottage where we stay sits above one of the many bays that reach their cold, salty fingers into the Atlantic Ocean. Standing on the porch on a clear day, we can see across to the tops of the two tallest mountains in Acadia National Park—the great, smooth upper reaches of Cadillac and Sargent. That all changes, though, when we walk down the seventy-eight wooden steps (I counted!) to the shore.

At sea level everything is different. What meets the eye is sky-colored water and, on the other side of the bay, a thick border of pines, birches, and firs. The mountain vista is gone and there's no ocean view—the ocean is miles away. Despite the expanse of the bay, it all feels enclosed and shut in somehow. Descending those seventy-eight steps lands us in a whole different place.

When I'm up on the porch and able to see out across the water and the intervening land to the mountains, my thoughts turn to exploring, to wondering what else is out there. I want to visit those far-off places. I want to know more. By contrast, when I'm down on the shore, my thoughts feel self-contained, more focused on what is right there. I study the rocks. I watch the comings and goings of gulls and other wildlife.

During last year's vacation I found myself wondering, "If I lived my entire life on the shore, if there were no way to stand on higher ground and see a view of something distant, what would my thoughts be? Would I have a sense of 'beyond'? Could I imagine anything different than what I could see from where I stood?"

As I pondered, I recalled a business flight to Indiana years ago. The fellow sitting next to me was griping about his experience in that state. "Midwesterners are so closed-minded," he declared. A bit startled by this random, blanket judgment, I asked him why he had this opinion. "The land is so flat and open," he replied, "they think they see everything."

It's been said that travel changes one's perspective. But it's not just that the places we visit are different. It's also that when we return, home no longer looks quite the same. Of course, not everyone has the money or the desire to travel. But is it possible that making a "vertical" journey as well as a horizontal one can accomplish a similar thing?

i find myself wondering . . .

Does the landscape shape our perceptions and thinking without our realizing it? Does it help our thought process to have some mystery and "not-knowing" in our surroundings? Some different vistas? How might we get a different perspective?

take a few moments to reflect . . .

Have you ever felt stuck or stagnated in one place?

Were you able to physically leave that place—traveling either "horizontally" or "vertically?"

When you returned, did you feel that your perspective had changed? If yes, in what ways?

25

sending probes into space

starting a project

Space has always fascinated me. As a child, I didn't have many opportunities to be outside at night, but I'd pore over star charts and connect constellations with the characters in the Greek myths I was reading. As teenagers, my brother and I would climb out through his bedroom window onto the roof of the garage to watch for bright, fleeting streaks of light during meteor showers. Lying on the slanted roof was easier and more fun than setting up lawn chairs—no craning of our necks for all those long minutes of waiting.

Now, as an adult, I often go outside late at night to look up at the sky. If I stand there long enough, I become almost dizzy as I try to grasp the vastness of the universe and the sheer number of galaxies and nebulas there may be.

I'm also enthralled by space explorations, amazed that scientists can launch a tiny craft laden with cameras and instruments, and chart a course for it that will take it millions and even billions of miles into deep space. It boggles my mind that I can hold in my hands images of such unimaginably distant worlds.

Part of what intrigues me about deep space exploration is how long it takes for these probes to reach their planned destinations. For instance, Voyager 2 traveled for 12 years to reach its far target of Neptune. Now, in 2024, 47 years from its launching in 1977 and long since free of the gravitational pull of our sun, the probe is still traveling, heading farther and farther into distant space. How many of the original science team working on that mission are still alive? Who will be reading and interpreting the data that continue to come in?

I often think about the long arc of projects like these, where a scientist working on the original idea may not even live to see the spacecraft launch, let alone see it reach its destination and begin to transmit data. How much vision must you have to engage in something with such a time span?

I think what compares most closely for the rest of us is bringing new life into the world. Hopefully, our children will live a good portion of their lives after we have passed on and we won't know and see all the rest of their continuing experiences. Similarly, when we plant seedling trees we do so knowing that we won't live to see them reach their own old age.

i find myself wondering . . .

What gives us vision? What makes a project worth it? Do we need to know that we'll see the end? Are dreams that go beyond us part of what we need to stay fully alive?

take a few moments to reflect . . .

What if you knew you had all the time in the world to start and finish a long-term project? Would you do it?

If duration of time weren't an issue, what would you do?

What would you most like to see or do in your life? Could you give yourself time? Could you start planning now?

NOTE: As of March 2024, the Voyager 2 probe had traveled more than 12.5 billion miles from Earth. Given that Pluto is a bit over 3 billion miles from us, that's a long, long way.

26

flowers along the creek

choosing our words

It's mid-March. Technically, it's spring, but the world remains dressed in brown and gray, and my eyes long for a splash of color. To satisfy my hunger, I watch the bird-feeders in the backyard and feast on the impossible red of the male cardinals, the fairy-tale plumage of the bluebirds, the crisp blue-black-white suits of the jays, and the glossy bits of scarlet on the heads of the woodpeckers and flickers.

Surprisingly, down along the creek, where the trees are still reaching winter-bare branches into a chilly sky, there's a carpet of yellow and green rolling out all along the streambanks and flood-plain. It's a groundcover called lesser celandine (*Ficaria verna*), whose bright, starry-flowered plants cheer the heart. At least *something* is blooming!

There's just one problem: this pretty-looking plant— native to Europe, northern Africa, western Asia, and

Siberia—is invasive here. In just a few years it's become hard to find any of the native wildflowers that used to bloom alongside the creek. Even worse, the celandine is now popping up in lawns and gardens.

To get rid of it, experts say you have to either dig it out while it's still just a small patch or apply glyphosate, the active ingredient in Roundup®. Digging is a challenge, and not foolproof: if you don't remove every little bulb-let, the plant will regrow. Glyphosate, well ... I don't like applying toxins to anything in my yard or garden.

So, I made a solution of vinegar and water and poured it onto the matted plants, enough to soak into the soil. I experimented on a few small patches to start, since I wasn't sure of the lasting effect of the vinegar. It would eventually leach out of the soil, wouldn't it?

Well, no. I asked a Master Gardener whether vinegar was a good option or whether it might kill the soil. "We don't recommend using vinegar," he responded. "You'll destroy the soil biome. Glyphosate is the way to go." Two months later, looking at the bare spots in my yard where the celandine used to be, I see that he was right.

We use vinegar every day in salad dressings. Yet vinegar can be a killer. We use words every day in communicating. Yet our words can be toxic—we often toss them out without thinking of their potential impact, careless of the damage they might do. Like vinegar on the living earth, the effects of our words can be long-lasting or even irreversible, leaving relationships lifeless.

i find myself wondering . . .

Hurt feelings can be hard to mend. Sometimes it's impossible to do more than achieve an uneasy truce. How can we use our words to make salad dressing rather than weed-killer?

take a few moments to reflect . . .

Can you think of a friendship that ended because of something harmful you said?

Is there some "oil" that you can add to the "vinegar" to soothe your friend's hurt feelings?

Sometimes the best remedy is simply saying, "I screwed up, and I'm sorry. How can I make things right between us?"

27

"esther williams" goes for a swim

making assumptions

⸙

The caterpillar was dead. At least that's what my husband thought. While I was out for a walk, Charlie noticed that one of the black swallowtail larvae I'd brought inside had slipped off the stems of common rue (*Ruta graveolens*)* and into the jar of water holding them. The larva lay motionless. Charlie gave me the news when I returned. "The caterpillar is dead," he told me. "I put it outside."

Saddened, I said a little prayer for this tiny, wild creature and then put the incident out of my mind. That is, until I went out a little later to toss the day's vegetable scraps into the compost bin. I noticed the jar of rue stems sitting on the patio near the back door. I picked it up and saw that the caterpillar was still in the water. What?

---

* Common rue is a host plant for black swallowtails, along with parsley, dill, and fennel.

I'd assumed that Charlie had fished out the larva and checked for signs of life. Clearly, he hadn't. For my part, I've rescued enough dead-looking insects from watering cans and buckets to know that when an insect is floating, inert, it doesn't necessarily mean that it's expired. Quickly, I poured out the water so that the caterpillar was caught on the stems. Was it my imagination, or did I see a tiny leg try to latch on?

I carried the perhaps-not-dead larva into the house and under a lamp for a better look. No movement. I started preparing dinner, checking on the caterpillar every now and then. After just fifteen minutes or so, I saw that it had moved and gotten its footing. Within half an hour, it was walking around on the plant stems as before and had resumed feeding.

I was happy, of course, that the caterpillar was still alive. But I realized that my husband and I had each made assumptions that could have yielded a different result. One, my husband assumed that the caterpillar was already dead. Two, I assumed that Charlie had attempted a rescue.

Here was food for thought. My first reaction was to want to take my husband to task for not checking to be sure the caterpillar was dead; for assuming. My second reaction was realizing that I'd made an assumption myself. Certainly, not all assumptions are tied to life-or-death situations, but asking questions and gathering more information almost always provides better results.

i find myself wondering . . .

Why do we so easily jump to conclusions? Is it a habit? A form of laziness? Or does it point to the ego wanting to believe it knows what the truth is?

take a few moments to reflect . . .

Can you recall a time when making an assumption turned out badly? What could you have done differently?

Has making assumptions ever yielded positive results for you?

Be extra observant over the next few days. See if you can catch yourself in the act of assuming. What's a strategy you can use to steer clear of that trap?

NOTE: Following this adventure, I dubbed the caterpillar "Esther Williams," after the famous synchronized swimmer. During her long career, Williams spent a lot of time in the water and emerged a winner.

28

sunrise on vero beach

greeting the day

Finally, it's spring—by the calendar, at least—and the days are full of sunlight. My introverted, raised-in-New-England self loves the quiet, dark winter months, but I also rejoice in the renewed quality and length of light. It brings a sense of enlivening, as if I am one of nature's creatures. Which of course I am.

On this bright, cloud-free day, I remember a business trip to Vero Beach, Florida. It was January, and even though I was there to work it was a nice break to be able to hang out in shorts and a tee-shirt after the business part of the day or go swimming in the warm waters of the Atlantic Ocean.

It felt like such a treat to be there enjoying the simplicity and ease of the weather. The Holiday Inn where our group was staying was right on the beach. Every morning on the way to breakfast, I'd make a little detour around to the back side of the hotel to watch the sun coming up over the water. I just couldn't seem to get enough of that beautiful, glowing expanse.

Every day that week, I performed this little ritual. And every day I wondered, "Why isn't anyone else out here?" I vowed then that I'd never let a day go by when I didn't open the bedroom window, or run downstairs and open the front door, and greet the day. I literally sing out a cheery, "Good *Morn*-ing!"

That simple practice lifts my heart, helps me feel connected to the Earth and everything on and in it, and, well, it just makes me feel good. In that brief moment of celebration—calling out a greeting and then inhaling a deep breath of the morning air—I feel a tremendous surge of gratitude. For being privileged to be alive on yet another day. For having a day in front of me in which to learn, laugh, love, and grow. For all the possibilities in a day just barely begun.

This practice blesses my heart and mind with the beautiful memory of those balmy days on the beach, far away from the cold, snow, and ice. Close to the rhythms of the earth. Close to my heart. And I find that it's almost as if I'm greeting myself. My "Good morning!" is somehow as much said to me as to the day.

i find myself wondering . . .

This tiny, brief practice helps set my mood for the day. Are there other opportunities where I can take a moment and reset?

take a few moments to reflect . . .

What's a currently "neglected" moment of the morning when you could pause for a tiny reflection—perhaps in the shower or with your first sip of coffee or tea?

How could you use that moment to set a mood or intent for the day?

How might that change things?

29

botanical rivals
moving up in the world

At the bottom of our hill there's a small waterfall that spills out of a neighbor's yard to tumble down a gully of layered rock to the creek below. Geologists call this particular expression of Triassic shale the Stockton Formation. (A geologist friend told me this.) The formation provides the scaffolding for the waterfall and also appears in a rocky outcropping on the other side of the road. I imagine that much of the underlying rock throughout this area is the same stuff.

In early spring a lovely little native wildflower emerges, perched in the bits of earth that cling to the narrow edges of the rocky outcropping. A single stem reaches up about ten inches from a rosette of slightly fuzzy leaves, then branches out at the top into clusters of small, white, star-shaped flowers. The plant is called early saxifrage (*Saxifraga virginiensis*). It's not super showy by horticultural and gardening standards; there's no big, eye-catching splash of color. And yet I love how these plucky little plants decorate the rocks.

This year, I noticed a new plant growing among the saxifrage. It's hairy bittercress (*Cardamine hirsute*), a plant that looks so much like saxifrage it's hard to tell from a distance that the two plants are not the same. Here's the thing though: the non-native bittercress is invasive. Able to shoot its seeds a distance of three feet, it expands its range rapidly. Sadly, it's now arrived on these ledges, where it's already starting to crowd out the saxifrage. But if no one notices the difference and doesn't weed out the bittercress, there it will stay. Soon, it will be as it if it has always been there.

Something I learned in one of my college courses is that within the strict classifications of the ancient caste system of India—a system much more intricate and nuanced than the familiar basics—there was an important loophole: it was sometimes possible to rise to the next highest caste by acting and appearing like a member of that societal group.

Imitation works for the bittercress and imitation can be helpful for us, too. I don't mean dressing the part to blend in. I mean looking at people whose positive traits we admire—for example, philanthropists, entrepreneurs, creators of all types—and trying to be more like them, putting our energy into useful, productive things. Or, modeling ourselves on people who are patient, kind, and generous.

i find myself wondering . . .

It's comfortable to hang around with people who are like us, but that comfort can make us complacent. Do the people you spend time with challenge you to make more of yourself and your talents?

take a few moments to reflect . . .

Whom do you most admire in the world, in your community?

What are the things you most appreciate about them?

How might adopting some of their traits/ habits make you a better person?

Do you think that you could be a more positive force in the world?

what's the end?

flowering like a tree

I wonder how many times this scene is played out every year: a homeowner contacts a tree expert and complains, "Last year, the tree was full of flowers. This year, it looks like it's dying. I don't know what happened. What's wrong with it?"

The homeowner expects that the tree expert will lay out a range of options, from ground feeding to a foliar nutritional spray, or that the arborist will pry a knife under the bark and display the hidden evidence of an insect infestation: "Gotta spray for that."

Unfortunately, probably none of those things will happen. Instead, the arborist will tell the tree owner, "Your tree is dying. Nothing you can do about it."

Right about now, the property owner starts thinking that they called the wrong "expert." "Aren't you listening? The tree had TONS of flowers last year! It's obviously not dying."

The fact is that a tree can sense when it's had enough—either enough years or enough environmental stress. In that season of knowing, a tree will put its energy into seed production to ensure that its genetic material lives on.

As I approach my 70th birthday, I'm feeling a kinship with these old trees. My friends imagine that now that I'm retired, I'm kicking back and enjoying lazy days with my husband. Instead, I've been busier than ever—in truth, a bit frenetic with writing, teaching, performing—and wondering why. I finally realized that what's at work is that I have no idea how many days, months, or years I have left on the planet. No way of knowing how much more time I have to spend with family and friends, to write, to play music, to paint, to hike and explore, to grow another season of vegetables.

To write . . . The angst hits hard there, as I question whether I can finish even half of the projects I want to bring to life. In my own way, I am that old tree, sensing that the end is not far off, and wanting to leave some enduring part of myself to the world before I go.

Botanists have discovered that an aging tree will share what it has with younger trees, passing along nutrients through an underground network of specialized fungi. I see a similarity here, too, as I delight in passing on what I know to my young students and imagining a promising musician enjoying the gift of my cello when I no longer need it.

i find myself wondering . . .

Is there a way that I can continue to "flower" without exhausting myself? Why is it so important for me to achieve? How much is enough to leave behind?

take a few moments to reflect . . .

Make a list of what you can share with the world. Try to not overthink this—let your heart speak to you.

Consider your list. What are the three things on it that call to you the most?

Pick one of those three. Could this be your great "flowering"?

appendix

Page 59

Birding is Fun's YouTube video:
 "Mud dauber making nest"

http://www.youtube.com/watch?v=BWr66LEqav0

Page 75

NoCamels.com's article titled "What Do 2,000-Year-Old Ancient Judean Dates Taste Like? Israeli Scientists Find Out"

https://nocamels.com/2020/09/2000-ancient-judean-dates-israeli-scientists/

about the author

Pamela Baxter has been exploring the outdoors since she was a child, turning to the natural world for enjoyment, inspiration, solace, and rejuvenation.

With a background in botany and plant taxonomy plus experience in her own gardens, Pam has been inspiring gardeners in the Greater Philadelphia Area since 1999 with her weekly column, *From the Ground Up*. Her articles span a wide range of topics, including organic vegetable growing, houseplants, landscaping with native plants and trees, creating wildlife habitat, Earth stewardship, and visits with local gardeners.

A contributing writer to the American Horticultural Society's *American Gardener* magazine and to *The Philadelphia Inquirer*, for 24 years Pam was the editor of the award-winning newsletter of the Valley Forge Audubon Society.

She is the author of *Big Life Lessons from Nature's Little Secrets* and *On Grandpa's Beach in Maine*, both for children. *Listening to Nature's Voice: Reflections on the World Around Us* is her first book for adults.

A cellist, Pam teaches privately and performs with a local orchestra. She also enjoys exploring our national parks, hiking, and cooking with the vegetables that come out of her organic garden in southeastern Pennsylvania, where she lives with her husband Charlie.

www.ingramcontent.com/pod-product-compliance
Lightning Source LLC
Chambersburg PA
CBHW031129020426
42333CB00012B/290